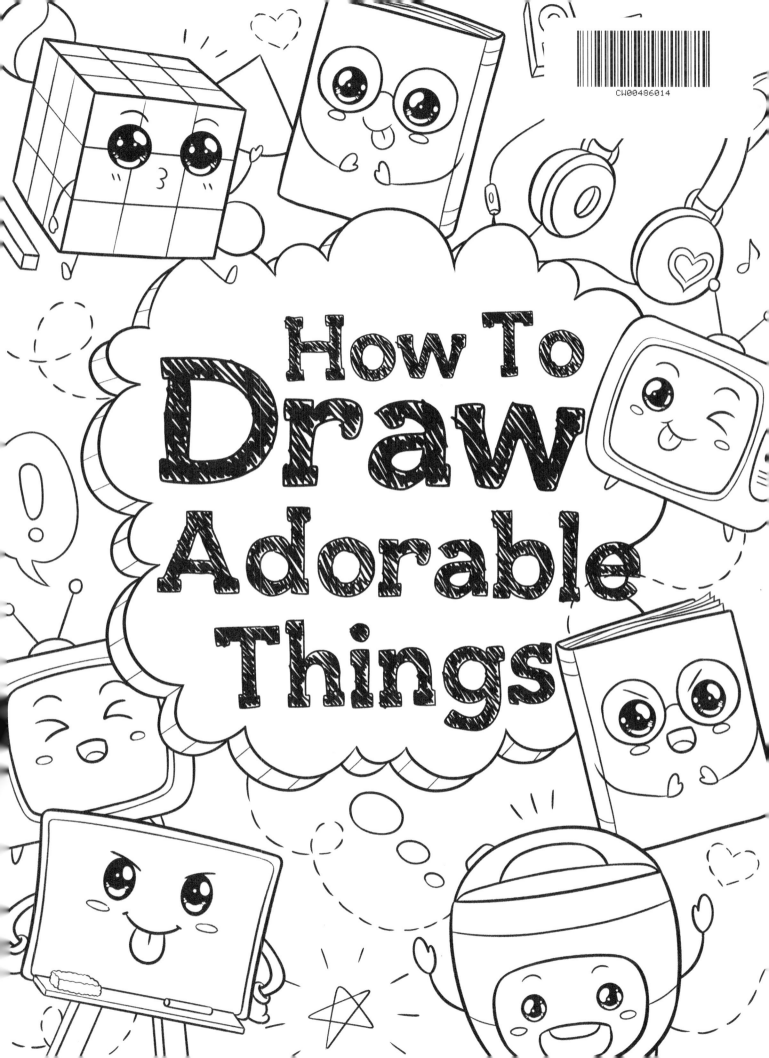

How To Draw Adorable Things

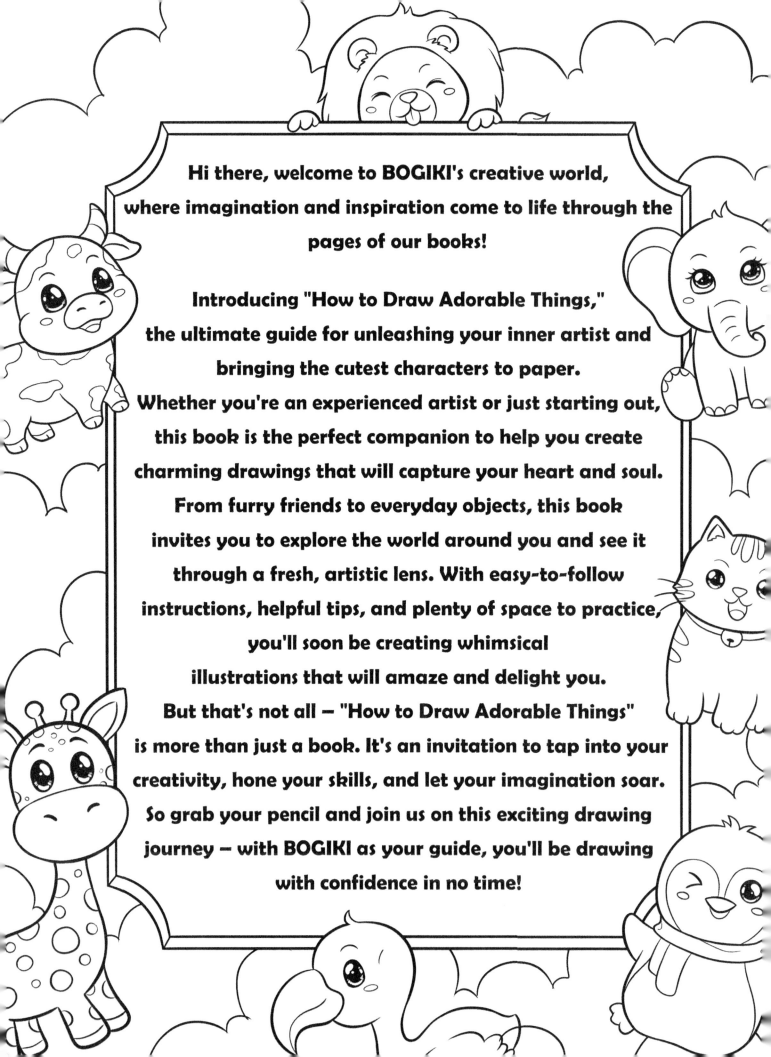

Hi there, welcome to **BOGIKI**'s creative world, where imagination and inspiration come to life through the pages of our books!

Introducing **"How to Draw Adorable Things,"** the ultimate guide for unleashing your inner artist and bringing the cutest characters to paper. Whether you're an experienced artist or just starting out, this book is the perfect companion to help you create charming drawings that will capture your heart and soul. From furry friends to everyday objects, this book invites you to explore the world around you and see it through a fresh, artistic lens. With easy-to-follow instructions, helpful tips, and plenty of space to practice, you'll soon be creating whimsical illustrations that will amaze and delight you. But that's not all — **"How to Draw Adorable Things"** is more than just a book. It's an invitation to tap into your creativity, hone your skills, and let your imagination soar. So grab your pencil and join us on this exciting drawing journey — with **BOGIKI** as your guide, you'll be drawing with confidence in no time!

WHAT'S INSIDE?

Bathtub

Comb

Bow

AirPods

Blackboard

Test tube

Syringe

Microscope

Earpiece

Stethoscope

Bandage

Thermometer

Scalpel

Pill

Wheelchair

Crutch

Brick

Gate

Hammer

Tape

WHAT'S INSIDE?

Washitape

Wrench

Bolt

Scissors

Wet towel

Tissue

Switch

Raincoat

Boots

Lipstick

Box

Candle

Desk calendar

Slide

Swing

Seesaw

Shawl

Rubik's cube

Yoyo

Snowball

WHAT'S INSIDE?

UFO

Table

Chair

Keyboard

Mouse

Laptop

Book

Ruler

Eraser

Magnifying glass

Key

Bucket

Printer

Roller skate

Handbag

Pillow

Mittens

Tie

Paperclip

Fan

WHAT'S INSIDE?

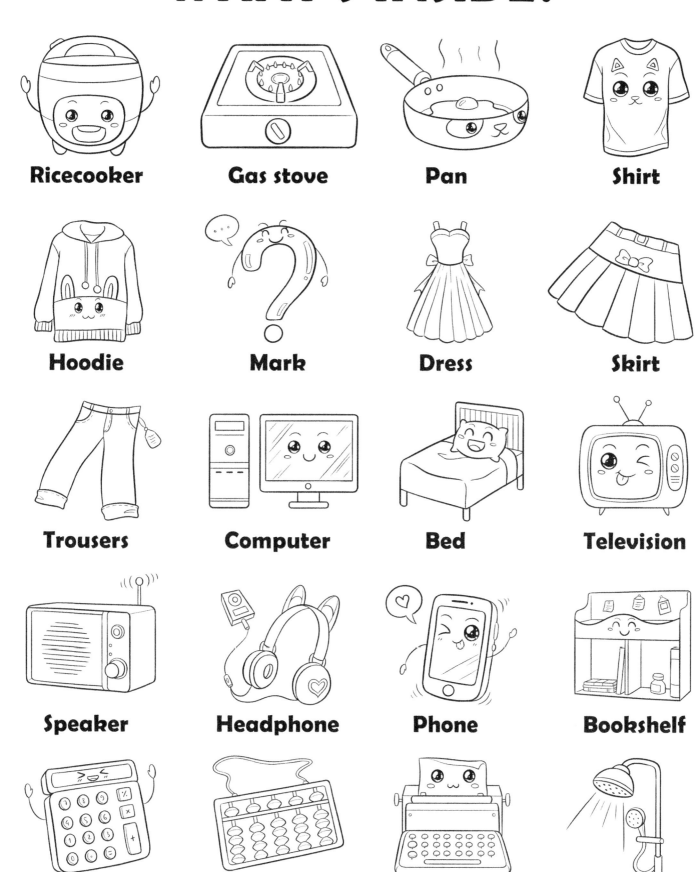

Ricecooker

Gas stove

Pan

Shirt

Hoodie

Mark

Dress

Skirt

Trousers

Computer

Bed

Television

Speaker

Headphone

Phone

Bookshelf

Calculator

Soroban

Typewriter

Shower

WHAT'S INSIDE?

Fox

Cat

Dragonfly

Butterfly

Hummingbird

Horse

Dolphin

Owl

Sloth

Penguin

Unicorn

Turtle

Shark

Elephant

Giraffe

Koala

Flamingo

Lion

Cow

Sunflower

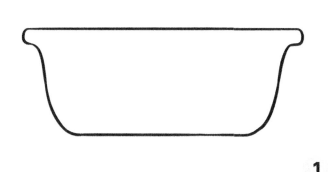

1

2

3

4

5

Practice

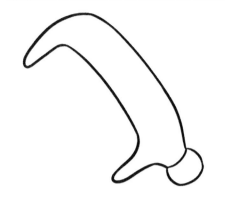

1

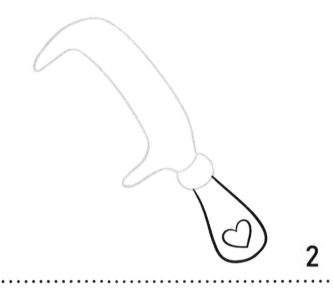

2

3

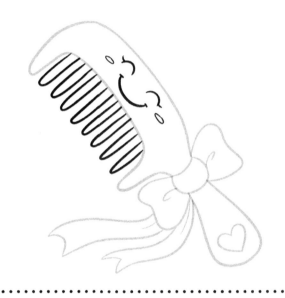

4

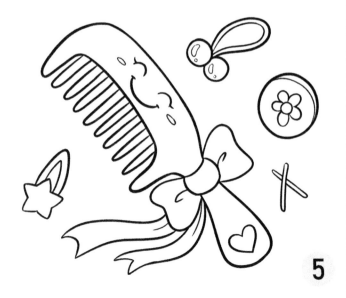

5

Practice

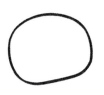

1

2

3

4

5

Practice

AirPods

1

2

3

4

5

Practice

 **Blackboard**

 EASY ● ● ● HARD

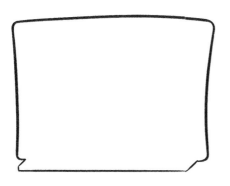

1

2

3

4

5

Practice

1

2

3

4

5

Practice

7 Syringe

EASY ● ● ● HARD

1

2

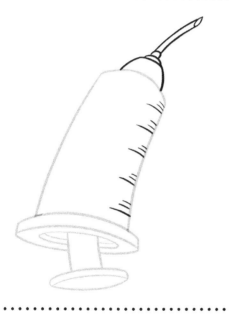

3

4

5

Practice

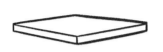

1

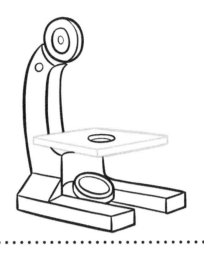

2

3

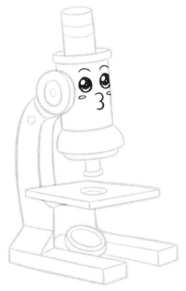

4

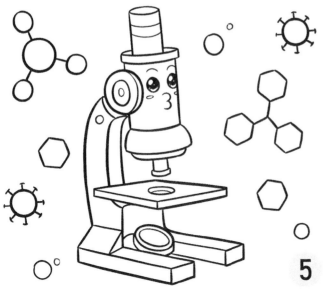

5

Practice

9 Earpiece

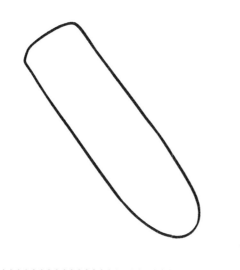

1

2

3

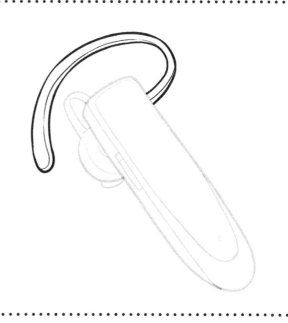

4

5

Practice

10 Stethoscope

1

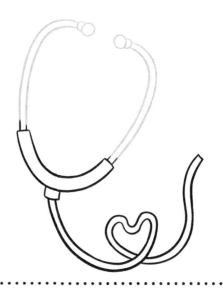

2

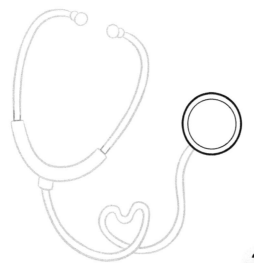

3

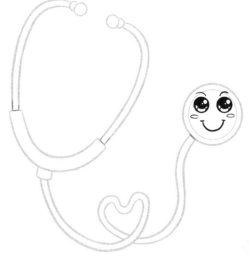

4

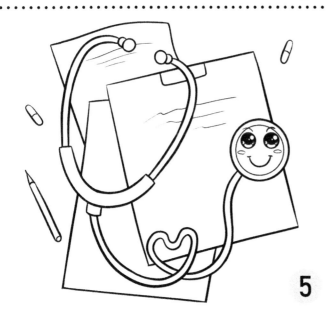

5

Practice

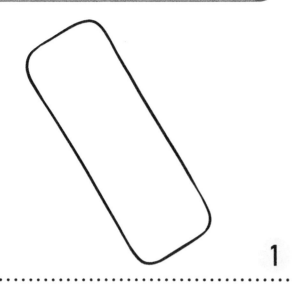

1

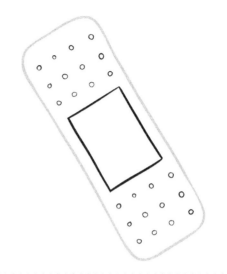

2

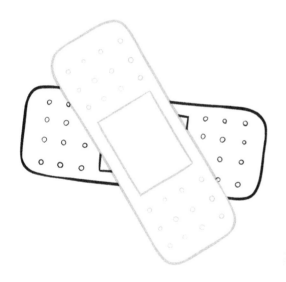

3

4

5

Practice

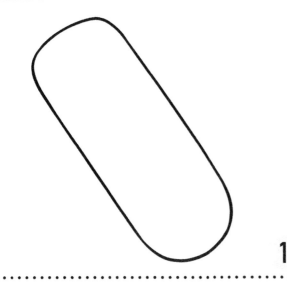

1

2

3

4

5

Practice

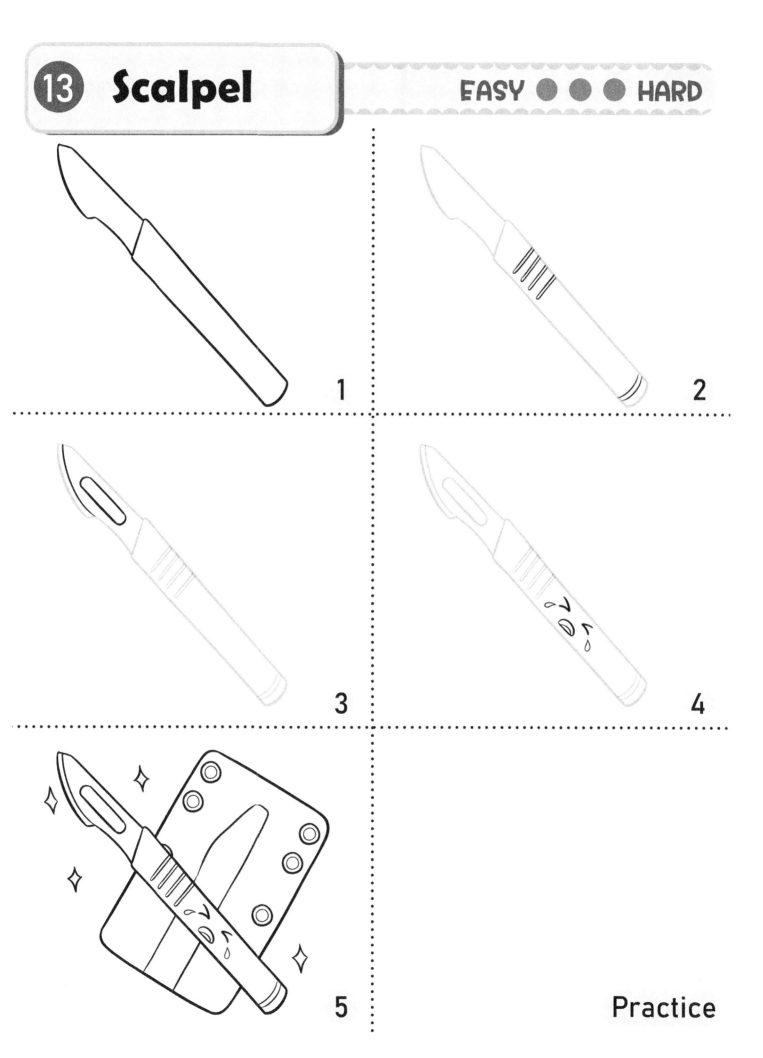

1

2

3

4

5

Practice

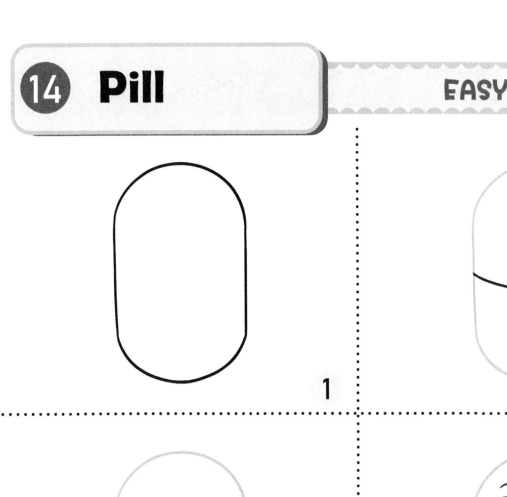

1

2

3

4

5

Practice

15 Wheelchair

EASY ● ● ● HARD

1

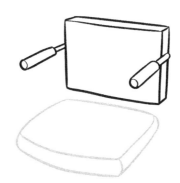

2

3

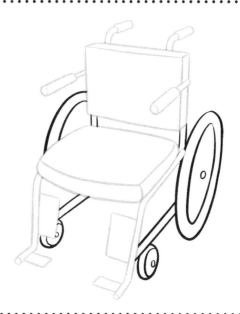

4

5

Practice

Crutch

EASY ● ● ● HARD

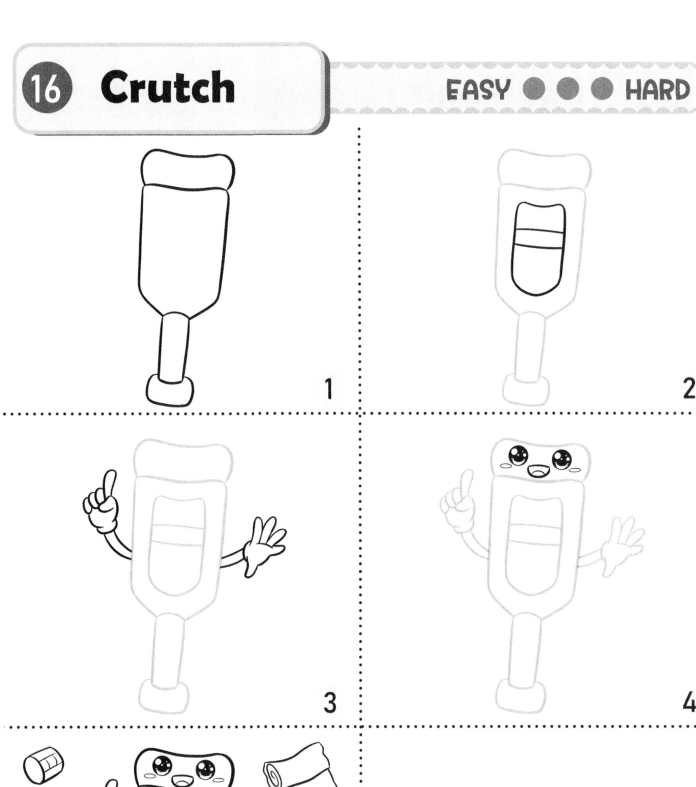

1

2

3

4

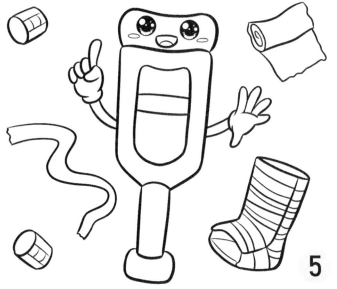

5

Practice

17 Brick

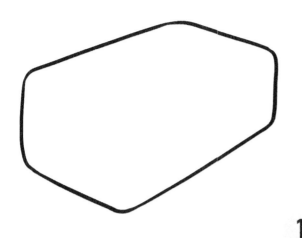

1

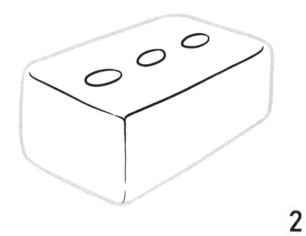

2

3

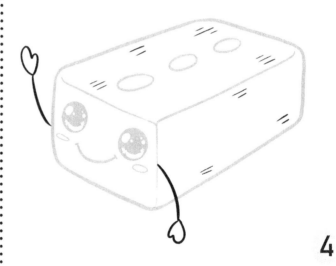

4

5

Practice

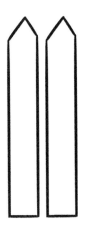

1

2

3

4

5

Practice

1

2

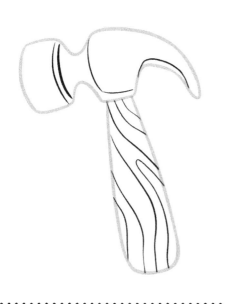

3

4

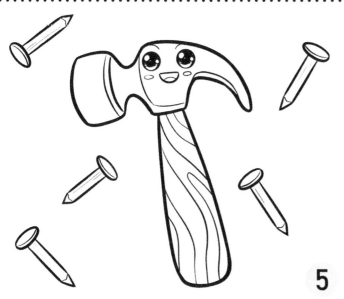

5

Practice

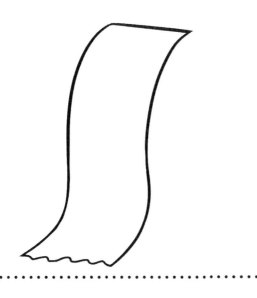

1

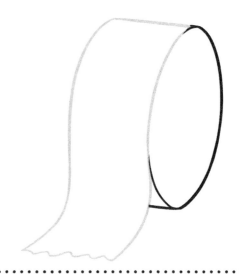

2

3

4

5

Practice

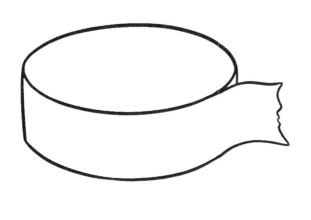

1

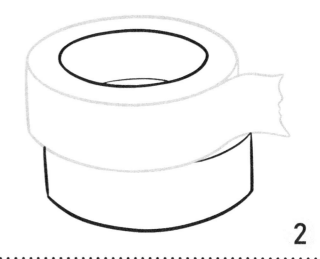

2

3

4

5

Practice

1

2

3

4

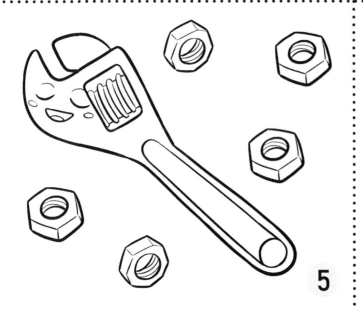

5

Practice

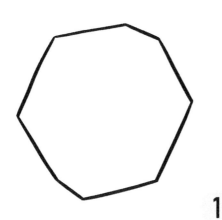

1

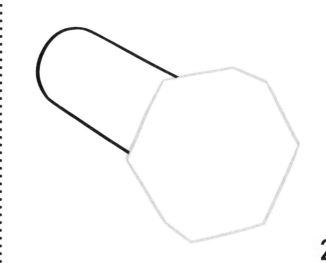

2

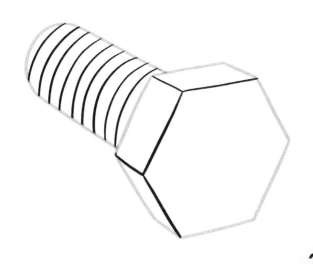

3

4

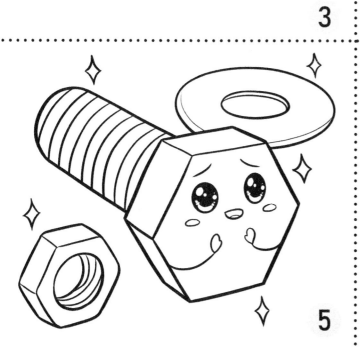

5

Practice

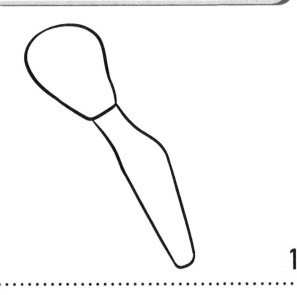

1

2

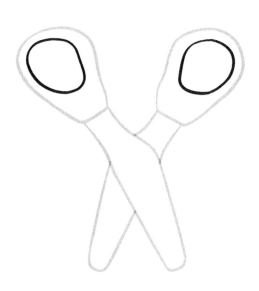

3

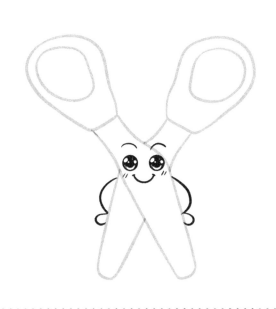

4

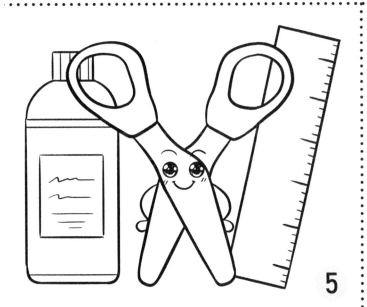

5

Practice

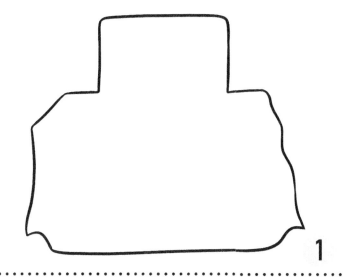

1

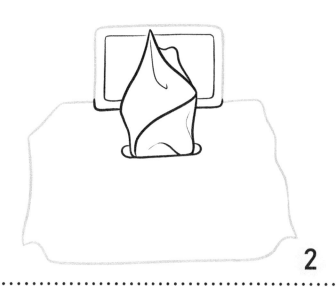

2

3

4

5

Practice

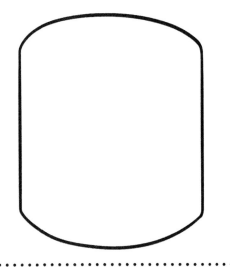

1

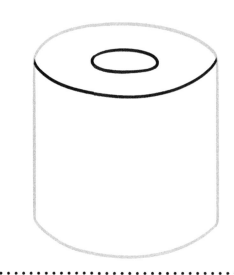

2

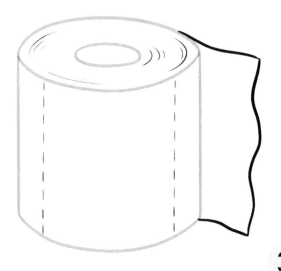

3

4

5

Practice

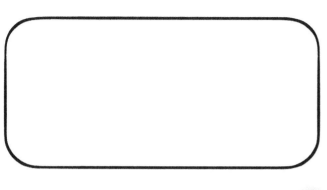

1

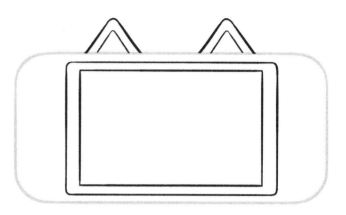

2

3

4

5

Practice

1

2

3

4

5

Practice

1

2

3

4

5

Practice

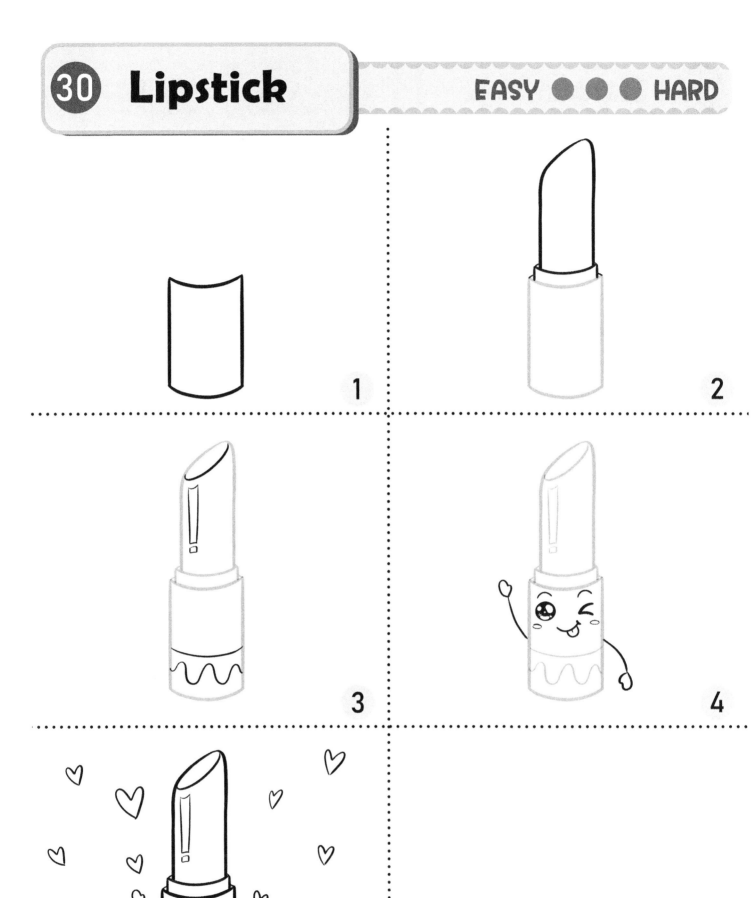

1

2

3

4

5

Practice

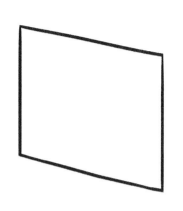

1

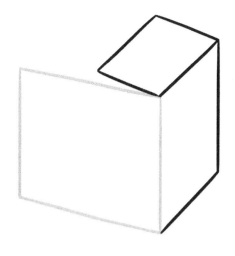

2

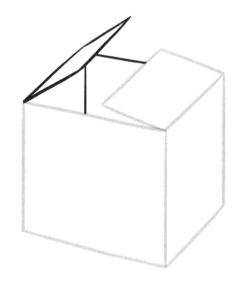

3

4

5

Practice

32 Candle

1

2

3

4

5

Practice

 **33 Desk calendar**

 EASY ●●● HARD

1

2

3

4

5

Practice

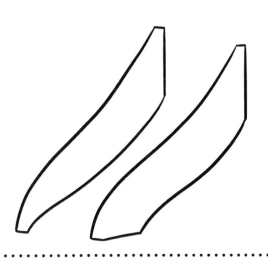

1

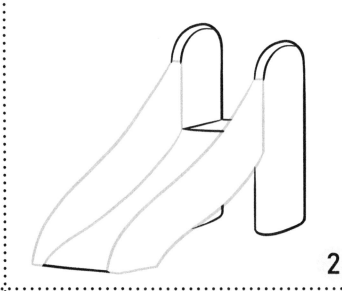

2

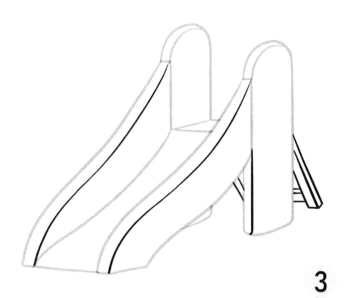

3

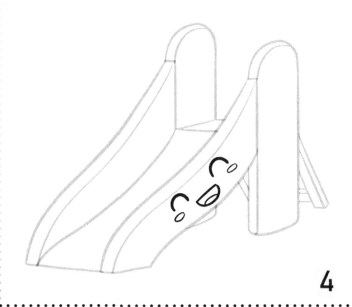

4

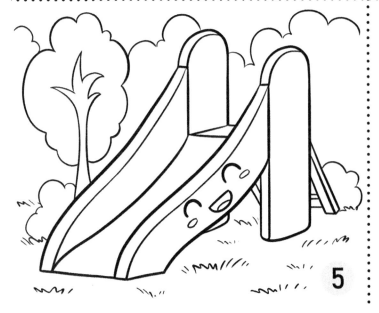

5

Practice

 **Swing**

 EASY ● ● ● HARD

1

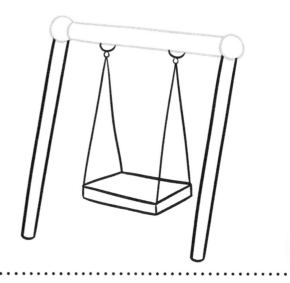

2

3

4

5

Practice

36 Seesaw

EASY ● ● ● HARD

1

2

3

4

5

Practice

1

2

3

4

5

Practice

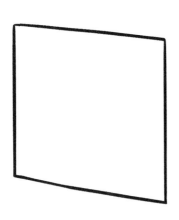

1

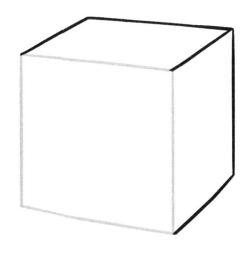

2

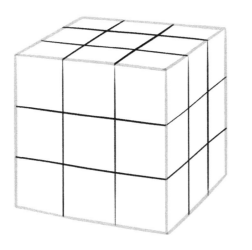

3

4

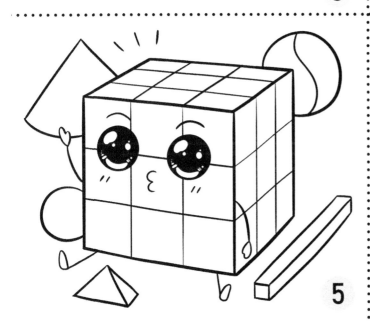

5

Practice

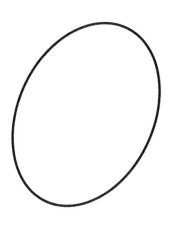

1

2

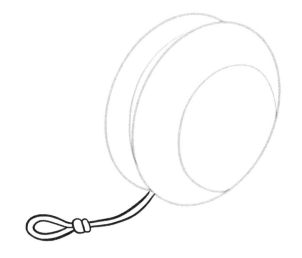

3

4

5

Practice

1

2

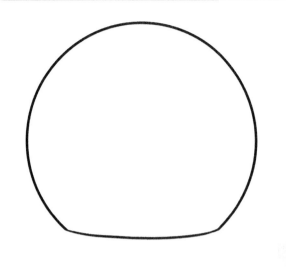

3

4

5

Practice

1

2

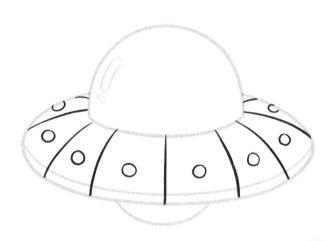

3

4

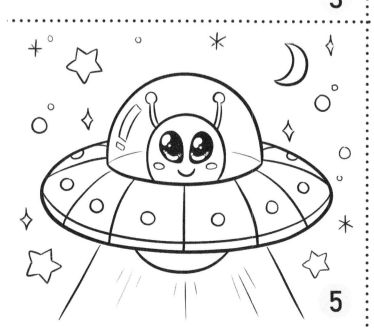

5

Practice

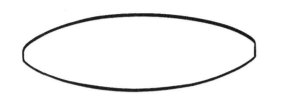

1

2

3

4

5

Practice

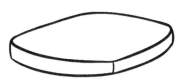

1

2

3

4

5

Practice

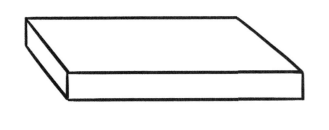

1

2

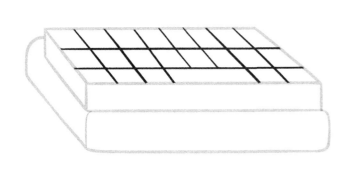

3

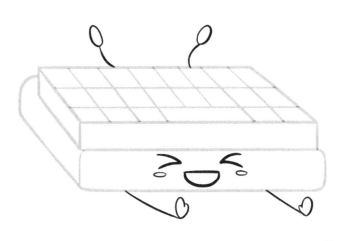

4

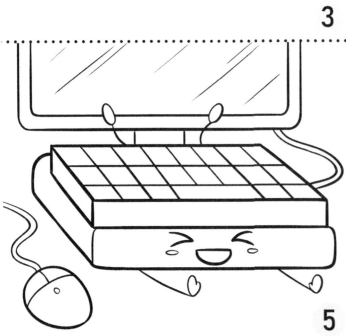

5

Practice

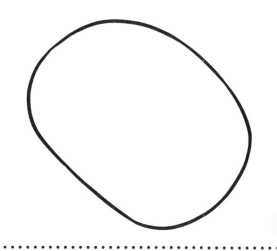

1

2

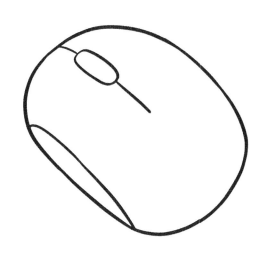

3

4

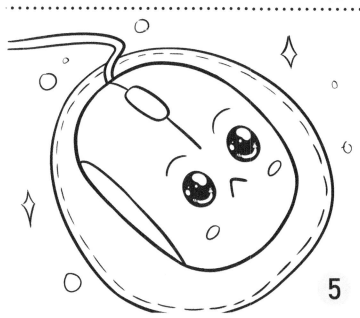

5

Practice

Laptop

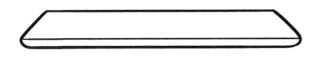

1

2

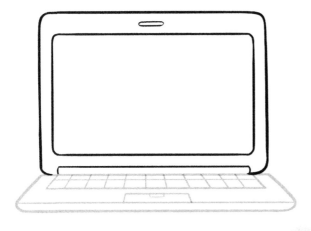

3

4

5

Practice

EASY ● ● ● HARD

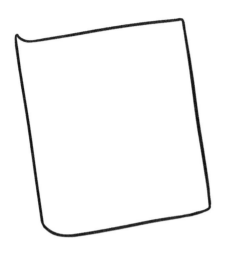

1

2

3

4

5

Practice

1

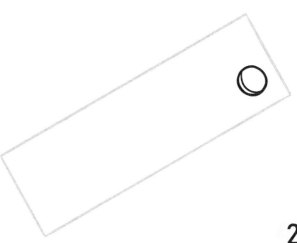

2

3

4

5

Practice

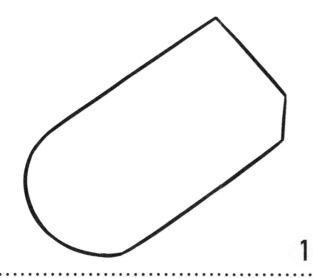

1

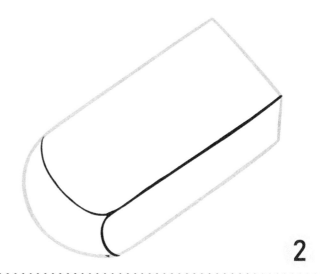

2

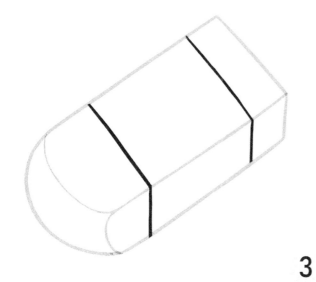

3

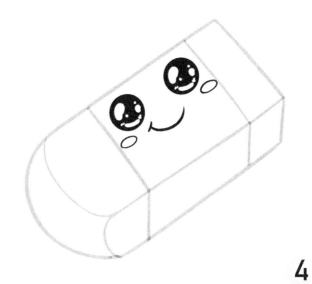

4

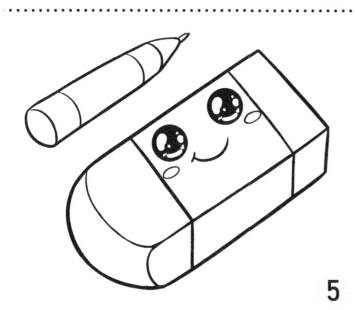

5

Practice

50 Magnifying glass

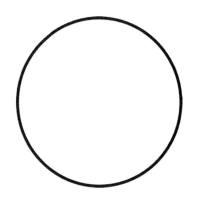

1

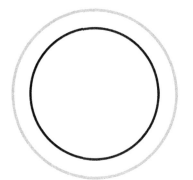

2

3

4

5

Practice

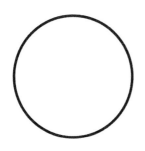

1

2

3

4

5

Practice

1

2

3

4

5

Practice

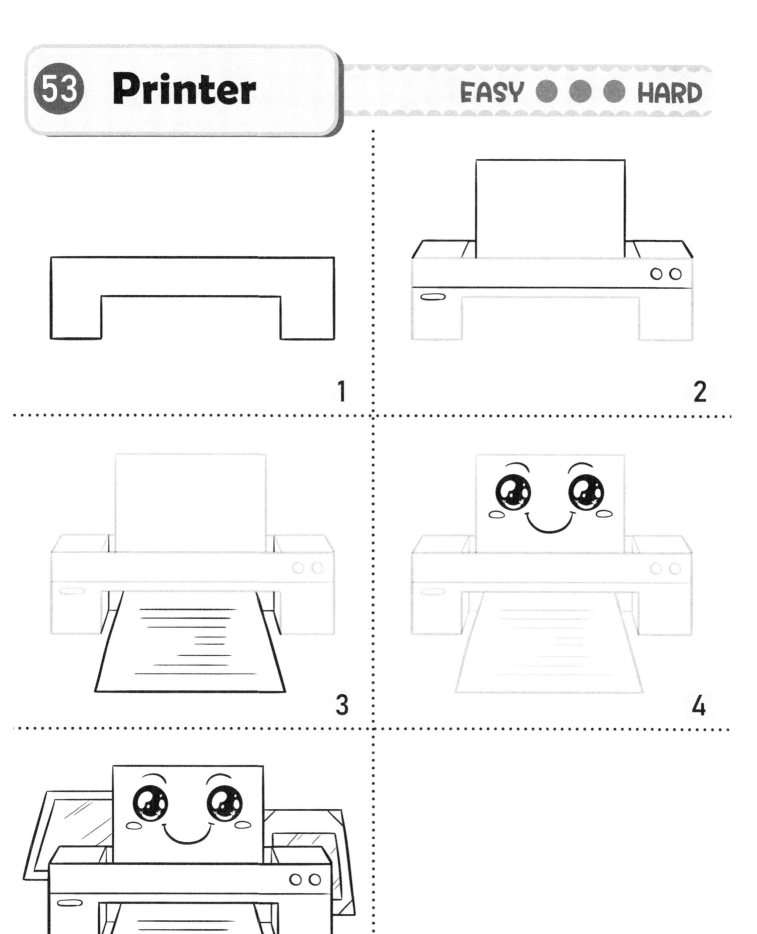

1

2

3

4

5

Practice

EASY ● ● ● HARD

1

2

3

4

5

Practice

1

2

3

4

5

Practice

1

2

3

4

5

Practice

EASY ● ● ● HARD

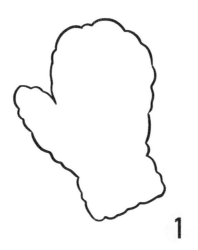

1

2

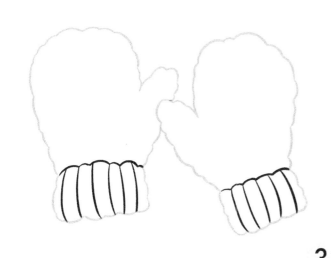

3

4

5

Practice

1

2

3

4

5

Practice

1

2

3

4

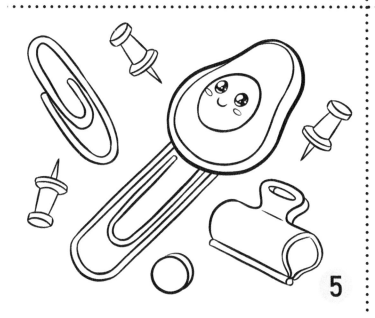

5

Practice

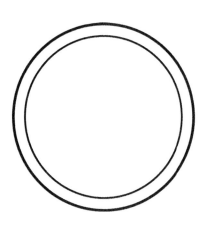

1

2

3

4

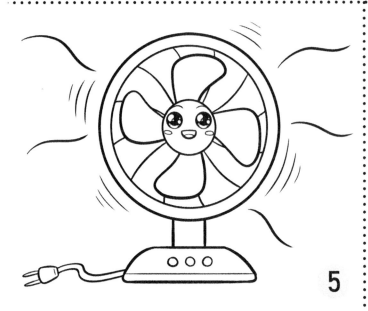

5

Practice

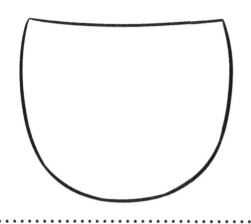

1

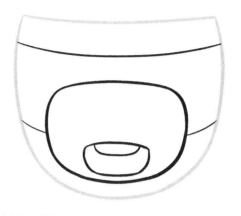

2

3

4

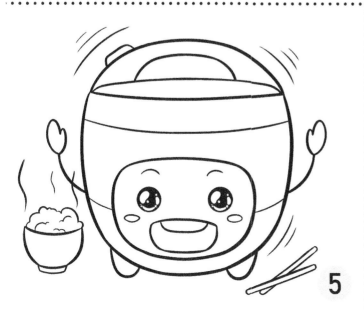

5

Practice

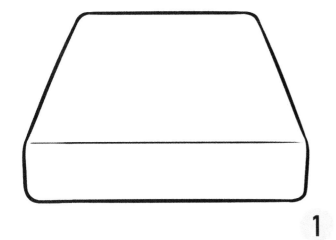

1

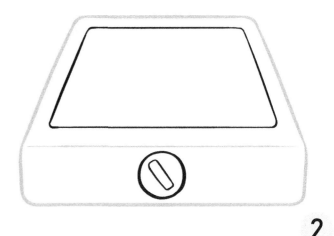

2

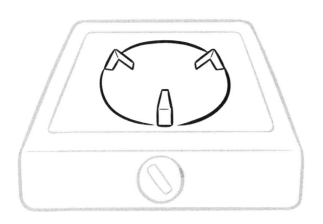

3

4

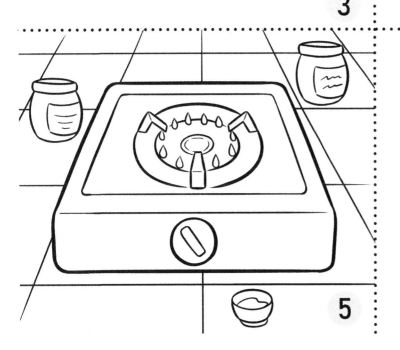

5

Practice

EASY ● ● ● HARD

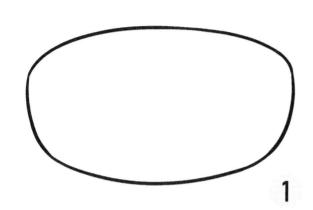

1

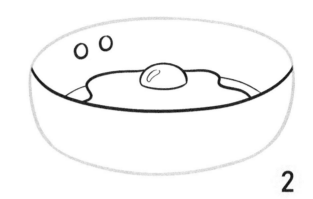

2

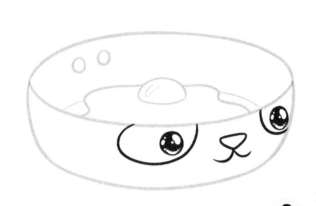

3

4

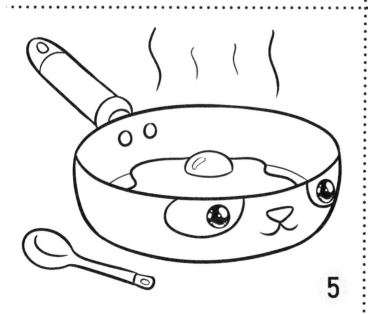

5

Practice

64 Shirt

EASY ● ● ● HARD

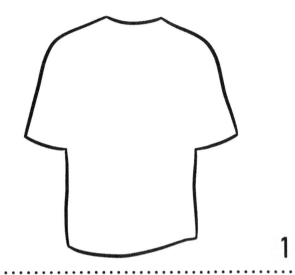

1

2

3

4

5

Practice

1

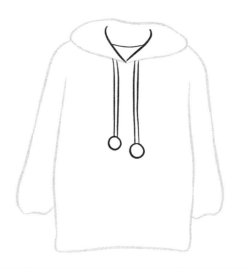

2

3

4

5

Practice

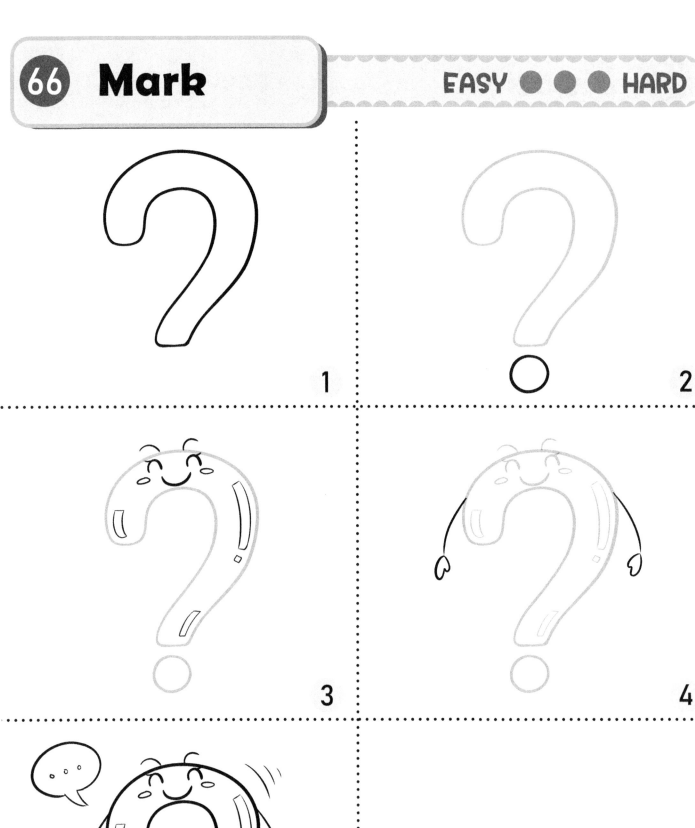

1

2

3

4

5

Practice

 **67 Dress**

EASY ● ● ● HARD

1

2

3

4

5

Practice

68 Skirt

EASY ● ● ● HARD

1

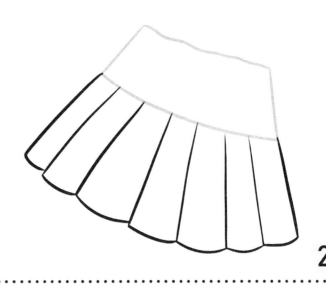
2

3

4

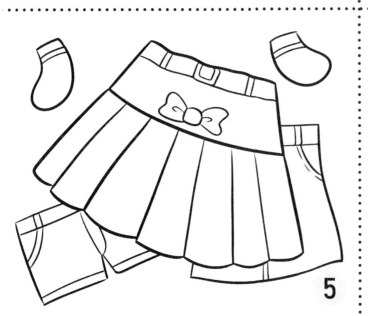
5

Practice

1

2

3

4

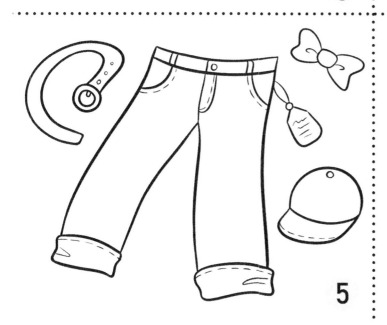

5

Practice

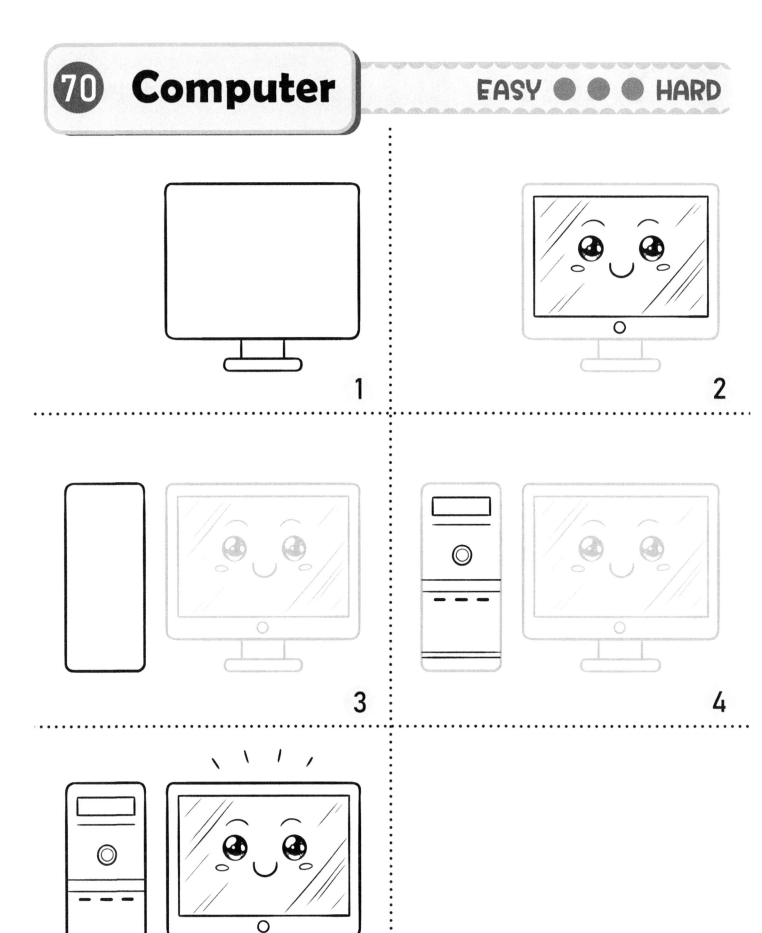

1

2

3

4

5

Practice

71 Bed

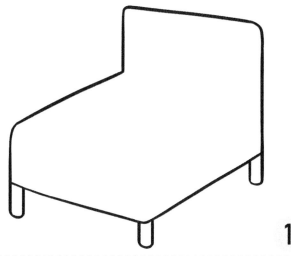

1

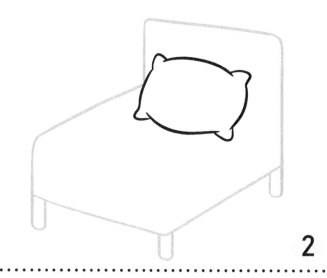

2

3

4

5

Practice

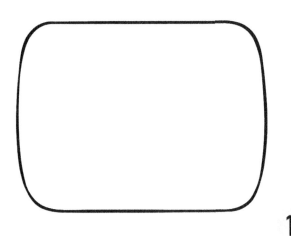

1

2

3

4

5

Practice

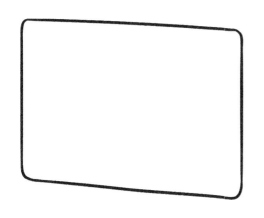

1

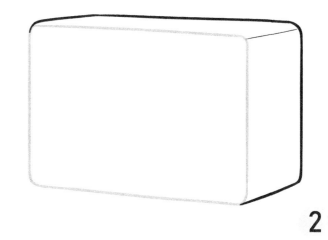

2

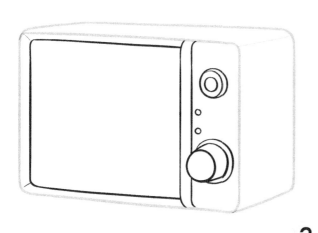

3

4

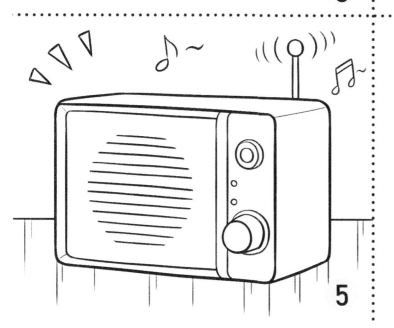

5

Practice

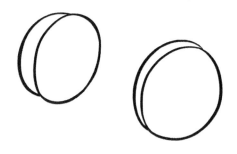

1

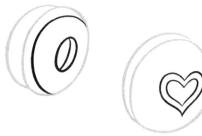

2

3

4

5

Practice

Phone

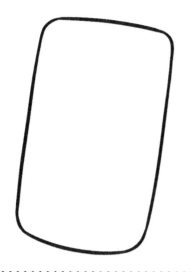

1

2

3

4

5

Practice

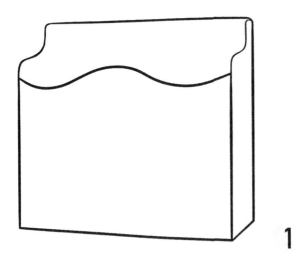

1

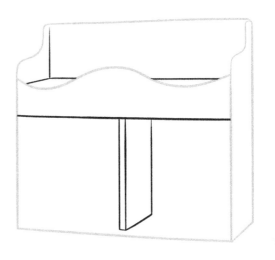

2

3

4

5

Practice

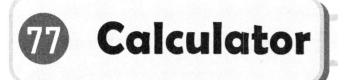 **Calculator**

1

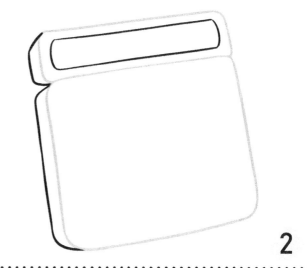

2

3

4

5

Practice

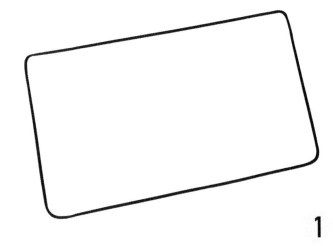

1

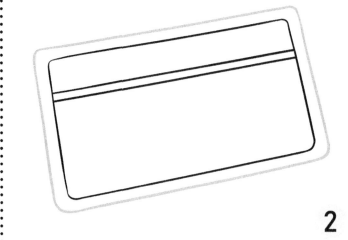

2

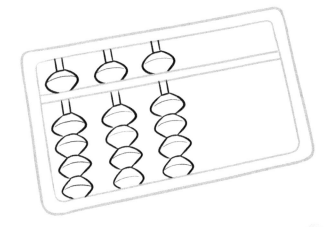

3

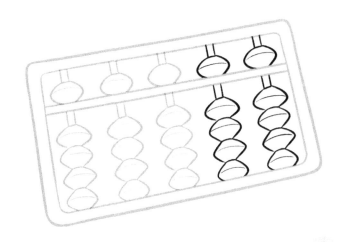

4

5

Practice

EASY ● ● ● HARD

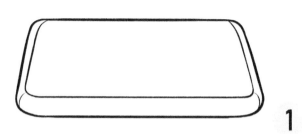

1

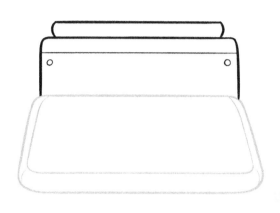

2

3

4

5

Practice

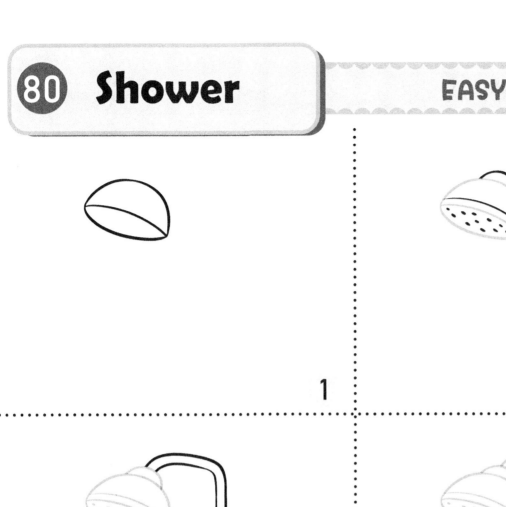

1

2

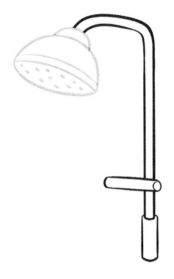

3

4

5

Practice

EASY ● ● ● HARD

1

2

3

4

5

Practice

1

2

3

4

5

Practice

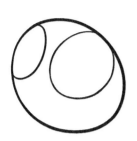

1

2

3

4

5

Practice

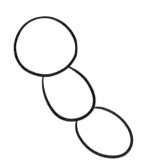

1

2

3

4

5

Practice

1

2

3

4

5

Practice

 **Horse**

1

2

3

4

5

Practice

Dolphin

EASY ● ● ● HARD

1

2

3

4

5

Practice

1

2

3

4

5

Practice

1

2

3

4

5

Practice

1

2

3

4

5

Practice

91 **Unicorn**

1

2

3

4

5

Practice

1

2

3

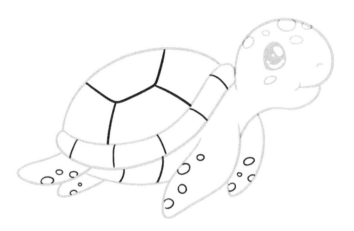

4

5

Practice

93 Shark

EASY ● ● ● HARD

1

2

3

4

5

Practice

94 Elephant

1

2

3

4

5

Practice

95 Giraffe

1

2

3

4

5

Practice

1

2

3

4

5

Practice

1

2

3

4

5

Practice

Lion

1

2

3

4

5

Practice

 **Cow**

EASY ● ● ● HARD

1

2

3

4

5

Practice

100 Sunflower

EASY ● ● ● HARD

1

2

3

4

5

Practice

Printed in Great Britain
by Amazon

31714769R00064